Wake up I Say! Live Life as if this is your Last Day!

Musings of an Appalachian Girl

Musings
Of an Appalachian Girl

Alex Hersom

Copyright © 2014 by Alex Hersom.

All rights reserved, including the right to reproduce this book or portions thereof in any form whatsoever.

ISBN:

ISBN-13:
978-0615964485 (Hippy Chicks)

ISBN-10:
0615964486

There are so many people I would like to dedicate this book to, but I would especially like to thank Patricia Steiner and Amanda Steiner for the gift of travel, Marti Hersom for having faith in me, and Erin Henry for starting my joy of writing.

Musings of an Appalachian Girl

Contents

Killdeer	11
Sandcastle	13
Alamo's Oak	15
The Bridge	17
Dandelions	19
Scared	21
Doorsill to Camp	23
Mermaid Scales	25
Sky	27
Mikie	29
Christmas	31
Appalachia Dance	33
Derecho	35
Harpist's Song	37
Pickle Jar	39
Bioluminescent Bay	41
Worry Doll	43
Old Medicine Bottles	45
Volcano	47
Peepers	49
The Clocks	51
Wedding Day	53
Aspen in Autumn	55
May Basket	57
Book	59
Ledgemere	61
Orchestra	63
Old Stone House	65
Rooster	67
Worker Honeybee	69
Grandma	71
Pearl Harbor	73
Bluebird	75
Jack Frost	77
Paul	79
Sunflower	81
Drive-in Theater	83

Contents

Clackmeisters	85
Home in Appalachia	87
Fountain of Youth	89
America	91
Blackwater Falls	93
Life's Ambition	95
Joys of being Seven	97
The Famous Architect	99
Grow Group	101
Origami Boat	103
Starlings	105
Grandma's Teapot	107
Song of the Gulls	109
Storm	111
Zak	113
True Friend	115
Morning Song	117
John and Isaiah	119
Children	121

Killdeer

admire the Killdeer
who tries its best
to sacrifice itself
before its nest

I'M HERE! I'M HERE!
to the fox it sings
darting away
with broken wings

though it would not
pay that fee
if it decided
to build its nest in a tree

Sandcastle

Our castle stands strong
Upon misty shore
Driftwood flagpole long
Rounded pine bark door
Molded by our hands
Oyster shells 'round top
Walls of gritty sands
Command winds to stop
Beyond castle tall
Sisters and I hear
Dragon's shrieking call
We tremble in fear
Pale wings above soar
We lower fishnet gate
It spins like a vulture
Alas! We're too late
Gull perches on wall
Causing it to crack
Onto us it falls
Sand doom is now back
Covered in sand grain
We'll wash off in sea
Then build kingdom again
For princesses are we

Alamo's Oak

towering, twisted
overwhelming branches sway
reflecting freedom

The Bridge

Two dairy farms beside each other
Were homes to friends with one another
Upon the frosted cold hill green
Crossing unknown land in-between
Sun rose dimly one early morn
As a special new calf was born
Rick's anxious brightening blue eyes
Like drifting wide open clear skies
Were first to see it up and roam
He took the calf off to his own home
"That calf there is mine!" Dave exclaimed
"Your wrong and you should be ashamed"
Said Rick with a face burning red hot
 "It's my prized calf, yours it's not"
Appalled he did not put it back
Dave slammed his barn door with a CRACK
Without glancing out to Rick's field
"From my acre his eyes I will shield!"
Dave said in a raging voice sore
Then hired an old carpenter
"I want a wall twenty feet high
Around my property lines!"
Though when the carpenter went out
He did not build the wall about
For he was brilliant and wise
And thought he'd take them by surprise
Stayed on the hill hammering all week
Dave never looked up at the peak
When finished he came down to show
Dave what lesson he had to bestow
Took him to his property's edge
To show him a long wooden bridge
Alone, Dave crossed what the man built
To where Rick stood with a face of guilt
Once Dave crossed to the other side

They embraced each other and cried
In your life, do not build a wall
Build a bridge to be used by all

Dandelions

Yellow bright the lion's mane
The only sun in the rain
Brought aboard as pilgrims' seeds
Now at home our garden's weeds

Scared

Grandma's balding head
exhausting leukemia
frightened yet, she smiles

i am Terrified
witness horrifying change
anointing the Sick

alone and helpless
Anguish. Lost. Fearing death
Scared- yet, I smile back

Doorsill to Camp

towering maples and fragrant pines
thick swaying limbs together entwine
arched over dusty road
glorious hall Almighty sowed
rounded green leaves wave hello
to tiny children far below
enormous trunks count endless years
watching them grow 'round their peers
soaring wild birds sing along
to campers' folk tales and song
feelings here I cannot explain
there is magic at old camp again

Mermaid Scales

when Grammy was a little girl
she went to wild shores of Reid
found what she called Mermaid Scales
and used them as necklace beads
tan, black, or clear the shells are
the size of a half-dollar but frail
gleaming in iridescent luster
though waves often crack them like shale

Sky

perfectly sunny
increasingly intense blue
earth's immense ceiling

Mikie

children are like new orchard trees
that, when abandoned, grow bowed
but you nurture and care for us
wherever they shall be sowed
lucky are we

Christmas

Fragrant tree, colors aglow
At last friends and neighbors know
Once again it's winter time
Gold church bells joyfully chime
The music proclaiming there
Is Christmas in the air

Down town roasting chestnuts pop
By gift stores with snow atop
You stop suddenly and sing
The caroler's tune that rings
The music proclaiming there
Is Christmas in the air

On hilly lawns children sled
In warm knit gloves blue and red
They mold a man of snow
While whistling songs we know
The music proclaiming there
Is Christmas in the air

With our high spirits leaning
Sometimes we forget the meaning
Of this time all about
Then it comes to us in shout!
The music proclaiming there
Is Christmas in the air

It is a time for giving
And for simply living
With family drawing near
It becomes easy to hear
The music proclaiming there
Is Christmas in the air

Appalachia Dance

celtic fiddle begins the song
jovially, folks clap along
one by one we make our entrance
round the circle, unison dance
making music with our feet
our hearts chasing rapid beat
we are majestically in flight
with double taps blissfully light
quickly clogging the turning vine
nothing on earth is more fine!

Derecho

Creaking walls Shutter
Flickering light bulbs Sizzle
Vibrating windows

Blackened Livid clouds
lightning bolts Fire like Guns
Roaring, Echoing

Rain collides with wind
Thrashing Shattering Terror
Relentless Power

Harpist's Song

her thin pale fingers
resemble a spider
upon its silvery web
that vibrates in musical waves
I am caught in song's trap

Pickle Jar

I'm carrying our large empty pickle jar
Mom gave to my sisters and I
So we can catch fireflies
Twinkling bright as a star

I lay our large empty pickle jar
In the dark grassy yard as we gaze
Three willow trees with fireflies ablaze
Twinkling bright as a star

Filling our large empty pickle jar
With carefully cupped handfuls of them
More beautiful than any priceless gem
Twinkling bright as a star

We take our large full pickle jar
Of twenty-three fireflies
Into our room now like a night sky
Twinkling bright as a star

In the morning we will empty our large pickle jar
Outside so that the fireflies may live
For another night of beauty they will give
Twinkling bright as a star

Bioluminescent Bay

Sunset dwindling
Kayaking narrow black creek
Up strong rough current
Canopy above thickens
Darkening chilled atmosphere

Air smells of sulfur
Waves hitting tree roots sparkle
Oars trail light blue stars
Boating across black night sky
Airborne though tied down to earth

Worry Doll

Fingernail-sized doll
You think would serve no purpose at all
Purple wound string shirt
Soft floral white cotton skirt
Black eyes, smile, and hair on its head
Children carefully take to bed
Whispered a worry late at night
Placed under pillow when off goes the light
Though useless the doll may possibly appear
It is a way for them to let go of fear

Old Medicine Bottles

The sun's rays peer on a cloudless day
Though antique bottles in a majestic way
Vibrant rainbows around the kitchen are cast
Stop and gaze as you walk past!
Deep blue, crystal clear, and green like the sea
Oh how old things still shine beautifully!

Starlings

great mass of black starlings
like dense chimney smoke
fly in unity as a gliding stream
conflicting frigid blizzard
ice like bullets strike their feathers
they hunt for shelter below
tall trees stand naked
they dream of emerald foliage

Peepers

Like beautiful birds they sing
On warm breezy nights of spring
And I; rocking in our porch's chair
Listen to their song sweet and fair
Oh how peaceful; hearing that tune!
Which awakens at the silvery moon

The Clocks

Silver was the pocket watch resting on the desk of wood
Feeling superior as she eyed
The dull corner where a sleeping grandfather clock stood
She watched as his moon dial flipped to the sun side
Creaking a yawn; awoken by his own sounding hour
The grandfather clock noticed her smirk
Stretching himself; standing like a tower
Aware of her arrogant thoughts; his number eyes became sharp as a dirk
Then, in a creaky voice, he declared
"What is *your* purpose? What is *your* cost?"
His pendulum rocked like an old man in his chair
"Is it not easy to be misplaced or lost?"
At her elder, the pocket watch gazed
"I can be taken anywhere; I have seen the world"
"*I* insure my wearer makes deadlines and meetings" she said ticking, unfazed
With pointed hands that slowly swirled
"What good are you?" she then did ask
In a tone showing her pride.
"Lifting you off your feet, why, two strong men must do the task!"
She huffed loudly as she cried
Once she finished her statement
The grandfather clock did not hesitate
He would not stand for this cruel treatment
And thought he would win the debate
"I've been passed down generation to generation
Never has my chime not heralded the hour
In this house it matters not your location
I can be heard by *all* throughout every room; that is my power"
They knew they were both right
Though they did not admit it and say
Their minds were wound too tight
How arguments waste time away!

Wedding Day

my white gown glistens
swans gliding on water
gracefully in ballet

Aspen in Autumn

Round leaves silky and flat
Gorgeous sight to be seen
Like dangling gold beads
Of a fair dark-eyed queen
Crowned in shimmering sun

May Basket

When Grammy was a young girl
She wove a basket in May
Using strips of pine with burl
For a special holiday
With penny candy; filled it
Went to home of a friend
Upon their door; lightly hit
Left it there; ran 'round house's bend
Listening closely to know
Once her friend had opened the door
To a May Basket down below
Then fast feet; her friend searching for her!

Book

embellished title
thin colorless pages bound
minuscule ink words
open your mind like a door
to world at your fingertips

Ledgmere

On small shore of Ledgmere
My sister Jessi and I play
Gray waves crash through the pier
Under hot sunny day
The seaweed tangled sand
Shimmers in rounded-glass blue
This is our freedom land
With abundant things to do
Through scratchy dark rocks we spy
Treasures in crevasses deep
Were oyster shells and star fish lie
And fast red hermit crabs creep
Jessi finds an old ship's wheel
Of driftwood we build a boat
Elizabeth Patrickson, Alice Keller
Pirate queens now we quote
Memories here we uproot
More valuable than any gold
We shall bury our loot
For we are pirates bold
Bury our memories here
On the salty beach they'll store
Someday they shall bring a tear
When discovered again once more

Orchestra

silent audience
dancing vibrations welding
Deafening Applause

Old Stone House

Stone by stone they built it
Many strong hands
Of a closely bound family
Four thread-worn
Floral cotton gowns
Mud stained
As four women
Sorely crouched
Unmeasured
Rustling wheat plain
Searching for large limestone
Three men, two boys
Drenched in sweat
Pounded blacksmith foraged
Chisels and hammers
To mold each rock
Similarly equal
Three giggly girls
Caked in mortar
Kept cool under wide straw hats
As they stacked stones
One on the other
Until the walls were too tall to reach
Worked dusk till dawn
Then spent humid summer and biter winter nights
Under wool knit blankets
Crammed on hard wood plank floor
Of a one-room log cabin
Until a cloudless harvest day
When the oak shingles were finally nailed
Atop the thick two-story gray mansion
Children watching in its long stretched shadow
Screamed and clapped with joy
When Father's voice echoed out

"It's finished!"
A week-long celebration was held
Town's folk who lent a hand
Joined the family
Camped outside
In white cotton tents
Around a great bonfire
Candles were lit in each window
Of the house aglow, bright and welcoming
Firewood smoke
From both mighty chimneys
Collided with white puffs from crackling fire
Flickering blue and orange
Dueling fiddles played all night long
By Grandfather
With rosy cheeks
And silvery hair under his leather cowboy cap
And William
The closest farmer; three miles north
With chestnut hair and a plaid-green shirt
Lively girls
Danced shoeless
Around the fire circle
Stories filled the perfumed air
Imagine
Tales which were shared
The house was strong
Two-hundred years
It never caved-in
Until the crawler crane's ball
Swung at it
Its silhouette
Is etched in my memory
Sometimes I wish
Companies would consider
The wealth of history
Instead of wealth in progress

Rooster

Large waddles and comb like a crown
Spurs like lengthy spears
Keen eyes and sharp head golden-brown
The ruler among his peers!
Cloak-like sickles black and blue
Ruffled scarlet feathers upon broad chest
Craning his neck he shrieks "Cockadoodaldo!"
Will he ever give the poor farmer a rest?

Worker Honeybee

Upon delicate petals
Of amethyst clover flowers
You collect nectar and pollen
Passing away busy hours

To towering white palace you fly
You are its protector!
Surrounding sisters
Share in golden treasure

And merrily the hive hums
In a song old and sweet
Until robber breaks within
A battle you must defeat!

With venomous dagger you stab
Through black tangled fur
But now your mind clouds
As earth becomes a blur

In sparing your life you saved
Queen; heart of the hive
Whom repopulates the colony
Again her kingdom will thrive

Grandma

there are people that see the light dim
with poor hearts sour and grave
but you have the heart of a vibrant gem
brightening gloom through a colorless cave

Pearl Harbor

Arizona Dark
Rusty, Incrusted, Mangled
Tears Flowing Up

Bluebird

Bluebird is bright
Swift in flight
Through the forest
And out of sight

Flutters though ranch
Perches on branch
Of knotty pine
Sheltered from sunshine

Hawk sees it from above
As a meal it would love
Swoops like a falling kite
...Then...

Bluebird is bright
Swift in flight
Through the forest
And out of sight

Jack Frost

Jack Frost is a whitesmith
Forging silver on trees
Elaborate skill called myth
Using water to freeze
Snow flies from his anvil
As he pounds the sledge of ice
Sculpting snowflakes with thrill
Delicate and precise
The bellows mighty wind
Chills frozen world down low
From his white cloud he grins
Watching children play in snow
Then his icy heart feels warm
And he sighs with frozen breath
Reflecting on life he mourns
Though he shall never sayeth
For without his gift he brings
Resting the world could not
Sleds would never drag by strings
Weather would always scorch hot
So he picks up his sledge
And forms beautiful art
Looks over cloud's edge
And feels warmth in his heart

Paul

painting vibrantly
using black and white keyboard
at your fingertips
swiftly brushing gorgeous notes
casting beautiful visions

Sunflower

Sprouts speedily
Birds share its seeds
Round brown face smiles seemingly
Unaffected by weeds

Thick green stem ever grows bold
Above other flowers like a tower
Stands proud, behold!
We should be like a sunflower

Its beauty always shows
Golden petals bright
Never faces shadows
Only sees light

Drive-in Theater

When summer opens the Drive-in
We are excited to go within
For it matters not what they show
We have a grand time when we go
The children play on swings long
To old tunes we all sing along
The scent of popcorn fills the air
Seated on blankets, weather fair
We play cards until the sun is gone
And cool breeze chills grassy lawn
Sound comes from our car's radio
Lighted beam begins the show

Clackmeisters

Members of church bell choir are we
Beautiful thing to hear and see
But it is even more grand
To be one at the stand
High arched ceiling echoes song purely
Playing in magnificent unity

Home in Appalachia

walking home from the school bus
on a worn out dirt road
the scent of dead leaves fills the air
a forest of Oak, Hickory, and Maple trees
Resting
Naked
Tall
their roots grip the earth

a red tailed hawk perches on a bare branch
it is Free
it flies where it likes
but always comes back to these ancient hills

my family has lived on this mountain
over a hundred and fifty years
like a tree we clench to this land
till we die and become skeletons, our souls
Resting
Naked
Tall
spirits whisper with the wind

soon I will make the choice
to be Free
I will go where I like
and know I will come back to the land of my ancestors

Fountain of Youth

I have seen the fountain of youth
In a cavern of Puerto Rico
With immortal powers declared truth
Though it is a mystery to behold
Trickling water sparkled as crystal
Weaved through ferns and orchids white
Volcanic rocks matted the channel
Peaking sun glistened upon it bright
And I had been one of the few
Who drank from the waters that day
Sipping from cupped handfuls I drew
Taking the legend with me to stay

America

Lest we forget
Seas to mountains high
The mighty eagle soaring
Through the fiery sky

Lest we forget
Fifty stars combined
A constellation greater
Than any other kind

Lest we forget
A river of tears shed
Stripes, red and white
For heroic soldiers dead

Lest we forget
This is the greatest country!
The gift being an American
Living wild and free

Blackwater Falls

as a lion roars
clear water falls like diamonds
reflecting orange sun
upon steaming blackened rocks
timelessly diminishing

Life's Ambition

My life is a trail God leads me through
Winding paths which I can pursue
Trees above shelter me from windy storm
Peeking sun keeps me dry and warm
But only God keeps me moving forward
My heart-woven dreams He leads me toward
When the shadow of night covers me
He is the shining moon so that I may see
When I get tired; journeying so long
He fills my soul with meaning and song
If I get the notion to stop and turn back
He is behind, urging me to stay on track
When my confidence bends or sways
He is my map; guiding me correct ways
If rocks and downed logs complicate the trail
I know if I follow Him I will never fail
He is someone on which I can depend
With me even when my journey comes to an end

Joys of Being Seven

birds chirp, fresh cut grass
blowing bubbles like rainbows
drifted by blue sky

The Famous Architect

Tim was a famous architect
Who was called upon by William
His old college friend had him set
To build a colossal mansion
"I'll give you money for material
Please pick out the finest supply
Do you best job, that's my one rule
I'll be away three months then come by"
And Tim said "I will do my part."
Though when William had gone away
Greed started growing in his heart
Wanting extra cash to be paid
He pondered over the design
Decided to create a cruel spoof
"Instead of oak I'll order pine"
He put warped shingles on the roof
Used cheapest floor tile he could find
Put in little insulation
At the slightest breeze the house whined
Then back he stood at his creation
Smiled crooked pondering schemes
Instead of screw he used a nail
Even the sturdy looking beams
Were split at center and would fail
The day William came back to see
The seemingly stunning mansion
He threw Tim back the silver key
And said "I forgot to mention...
This is my gift which I give you!"
When we have a job to finish
Great work for others we should do
And not be blinded selfish

Grow Group

Every year back I go
To this old wooden porch plain
Where I watched my dear friends grow
And I feel young again
Memories fill the air
Like bluebird's melody pure
In words it would declare
Past stories I vaguely remember
Though feelings here do not erase
No matter the years gone by
Laughter and smiles I can retrace
And it makes me blissfully cry

Origami Boat

The paper boat floats down stream
Setting sails into a child's dream
Dodging maple leaf pointy sharp
Like toothy jaw of a killer shark
And when at last it springs a leak
The child looks down sad and bleak
Though disappointment becomes light
When he folds a ship again right

Volcano

Looking down inside
Blackened
Steam gently rising from the middle

Surrounding trees are skeletons
Burnt
Lifeless above

Boiling earth churning
Scorched
Sulfur burns your eyes

Twenty years later
Green
Flora blooms with life

Grandma's Teapot

Grandma's silver pot
Whistles as water steams hot
Then around the table in company
We converse, enjoying a fine cup of tea

The Song of the Gulls

Breathe salty mist in the air
Feel cool breeze through your hair
Smell seaweed ashore drying
Hear waves crash and sea gulls crying
They're crying FREEDOM! FREEDOM! As they soar
That's all they know they never ask for more

Watch them dive into waves of the sea
Floating and calling gaily
Resting on sandstones ashore, drying
Hear waves crash and sea gulls crying
They're crying FREEDOM! FREEDOM! As they soar
That's all they know they never ask for more

Breathe salty mist in the air
Feel cool breeze through your hair
Smell seaweed ashore drying
Hear waves crash and sea gulls crying
They're crying FREEDOM! FREEDOM! As they soar
That's all they know they never ask for more

When your heart is full of woe
Remember life as sea gulls know
Go down to the ocean where your lesson's lying
Hear waves crash and sea gulls crying
They're crying FREEDOM! FREEDOM! As they soar
That's all they know they never ask for more

Breathe salty mist in the air
Feel cool breeze through your hair
Smell seaweed ashore drying
Hear waves crash and sea gulls crying
They're crying FREEDOM! FREEDOM! As they soar
That's all they know they never ask for more

Storm

dark gray clouds
rolling in
like high tide
of an angry sea
crashing thunder
thrashing waves
of icy raindrops
bitter wind lashes
lightning bolts flare
until the tide rolls back
and peace reigns

Zak

Dearest Little Brother
You have a great imagination
Each bright new morning
Awaits your every creation

You roam outside in bare feet
For they are clad in finest leather
Over your thick silvery mail
You wear a cape of heather

Tying thin straw you fashion
A thick noble gold crown
You are the king of the forest!
Building your castle round

Using dead logs you construct
Thick strong handsome walls
A shield from the howling wolf!
You stack one upon the other tall

You look out of the crevice
As you hear its horrible cry
And see its dark figure
Quickly, quickly drawing nigh

You are the king of the forest!
You are not afraid!
For it is only your little puppy
The adventure he will aid

A True Friend

a True Friend is like a candle lit
in gloom a beacon of golden flame
though it may flicker and whirl and cease
Love shall alight it once again

Morning's Song

sun slowly rises over shadowed grassy horizon
buzzing, honeybee lands gracefully in the center
of an unfolding daylily orange like drifting clouds
mourning dove coos its melody
sunshine peeks over fragrant pines
casting soft yellow rays
upon the colorful flower garden
ruby hummingbird
dips its long hooked beak
in red trumpet creeper blooms
little girl with a grass stained sky-blue dress
crosses her dirty bare feet
as she plucks silk white daises
placing them around her gold straw hat
whistling to
grass bending in waves
that crash at her legs
brunette hair flies past her shoulders
as wind suddenly gains strength
like a dam unleashed
millions of pine needles rustle
as if an orchestra, suddenly played in forte
the excited audience rose
the girl's gown swirls
dancing along

John and Isaiah

without a care for fame,
and wealth to bestow your name,
together you fill the room with guitar's song
bringing joy to all who come along
how wonderful is its simplicity
selflessly filling the air with beauty

Children

They see our world's beauty
Oblivious to its cruelty
Eager for each morning's rise
Awakening with bright eyes
Together they play
Spending joyful hours away
Their imaginations flowing
With creations ever growing
Learning right from wrong
Filling air with laughter and song
Small children we should envy
For they are wild and free

www.ingramcontent.com/pod-product-compliance
Lightning Source LLC
LaVergne TN
LVHW021356080426
835508LV00020B/2297